Sieon C. Roberts, Sr.

DISCIPCLESHIP
The Catch with Coaching Christians

DISCIPLESHIP, *The Catch with Coaching Christians*

© Copyright 2019 Sieon C. Roberts, Sr.

DISCIPLESHIP
The Catch with Coaching Christian

All rights reserved. No portion of this book may be reproduced, scanned, stored in a retrieval system, transmitted in any form or by any means – electronically, mechanically, photocopy, recording or any other – except for brief quotation in printed reviews, without the written permission of the publisher. Please do not participate in or encourage piracy of copyrighted materials in violation of the author's rights. Purchase on authorized editions.

Published by Literacy in Motion
Phoenix, Arizona
www.AnthonyThigpen.com

Anthony KaDarrell Thigpen
Editor-in-Chief

Library of Congress Cataloging-in-Publication Data Publisher and Printing by Literacy in Motion
Cover Design by Literacy in Motion Design Team

DISCIPLESHIP
The Catch with Coaching Christians
ISBN: 978-1-7336583-0-0

Christian/Self-Help
Printed in the United States of America

DISCIPLESHIP, *The Catch with Coaching Christians*

DISCIPLESHIP
Sieon C. Roberts, Sr.
The Catch with Coaching Christians

Acknowledgements & Dedication

I would like to acknowledge my loving and faithful wife, Lady Anita Roberts and my children Giara, Leon, Sieon Jr. and Jeremiah, as well as my granddaughter Amyra. To my mom, Delpha Roberts. my sisters, Hawah, and Arkeya, thank you all for loving me unconditionally.

Thank you to my publisher & friend, even more like a brother, Anthony KaDarrell Thigpen of Literacy in Motion. You are the one that has pushed, coached, and helped produced every publication and pieces of literature about my life. You are responsible for all the many newspaper articles, 4 books and countless professional photographs. I'm so thankful for your friendship and your unfailing acts of kindness toward me.

This book is dedicated to the faithful disciples I have the privilege of being planted amongst; the awesome people of the New Hope Church. Thank you for your tireless work in our branch of the kingdom, especially those that come to our Bible teachings. I would also like to dedicate this to the lead disciples that help me lead, our associate pastors of New Hope Church, Pastor Tim Grayson, Pastor Ellis Dumas, Pastor Christopher

Robinson, Pastor Rita Williams, Pastor Kewin Mabon and Pastor Anthony Owens.

Lastly, I dedicate this book to the one who disciples me, my father in the gospel, Archbishop William Hudson, III. Thank you for your love, correction teaching and impartations. You have been a true, pure and consistent leader in my life.

Table of Content

Introduction / p. 9 - 11
What's the Catch

Chapter 1/ p. 12 - 20
The Art of Discipleship
How Beautiful Are Their Feet

Chapter 2/ p. 21 - 28
Transformation of a Disciple
Fishermen to Fishers of Men

Chapter 3/ p. 29 - 36
You Are Not Alone
The Great Commission

Chapter 4/ p. 37 - 44
Assignment of Discipleship
Gap Fillers

Chapter 5/ p. 45 - 51
Characteristics of a Disciple
Conquering the Climb

Chapter 6/ p. 52 - 60
Examination of a Disciple
Staying Spiritual in the Storm

Introduction
WHAT'S THE CATCH

Discipleship is the defining role and most basic principle of Christianity. Throughout the 6 chapter of this book, "**DISCIPLESHIP**, *The Catch with Coaching Christians*", every reader should expect to experience a journey that will chronicle challenges and triumphs of being a disciple. Most of go to church services, but the Christian challenge is consistently sitting at the feet of Jesus.

Throughout my life, I've had the privilege of coaching many kids in four different sports. Its just as common for me to be called coach as it is to be referred to as Bishop. One day, my Bishop, William Hudson, III, enlightened me to understand that my coaching is not an extra curricular activity, but my destiny.

Readers will visualize a correlation between my secular coaching experiences to my discipleship enrichment training. Essentially, God expects us to duplicate in others what he has done in us. That can be equally intimidating for both the new convert and the one coaching them into discipleship.

This book will serve as a constant reminder of the steps needed to live and work for Christ outside the corporate worship experience. Here's the catch, many Christians or churchgoers are not prepared, nor interested in engaging in a deeper commitment. As a result, motivating and inspiring believers to engage in maximum performance is not easy. However, "Nothing great comes easy, and nothing easy can ever equate to greatness" (unknown author). Discipleship is not an act of going above and beyond the call of duty, it's our reasonable service. The following coaching techniques will help believers avoid the difficulties, disappointments and distract us from unwanted injuries.

> **CHRIST COACHING TIP**
>
> **DYNAMIC WARM-UPS:**
> Incorporate stretching with warm-ups. It gets the blood flowing and body temperatures rise. Warm-ups also get your body loose at the same time. This process gets us ready for maximum performance.

Chapter 1
THE ART OF DISCIPLESHIP
How Beautiful Are Their Feet

Discipleship is an art form. Art is the expression or application of human creative skill. It produces works to be appreciated primarily for beauty. The Bible explains the art of discipleship this way, "How beautiful are the feet of them that preach the gospel of peace, and bring glad tidings of good things" (Romans 10:15). Your desire to duplicate in others what Christ has done in you is a priceless work of art.

In essence, every believer brings their own sense of personality toward winning souls for Christ. It's often said, "People don't care what you know until they know that you care." As fishers of men, our personality has a lot to do with how we win souls to Christ. "He who wins souls is wise" (Proverbs 11:30). Our willingness, vulnerability and selflessness are the characteristics of love we use to win lost souls – Christ is the bait.

Everyone who has accepted Christ as Lord and Savior is commissioned to make disciples of others. Unfortunately, the church has strayed away from making discipleship a priority. Secular principles of prosperity, business, and motivational strategies have undermined the biblical doctrine of discipleship. The church is a body, not a business; it is a living organism, not an organization. Disciples are a body of believers appointed with the responsibility to spread the living word of God. We plant and water, but only God brings the increase. Growth happens organically in the kingdom of God.

Growth comes natural. The question is not how we grow, much rather, why aren't we growing? According to Matthew chapter 16, Christ promised that he will build his church. It is important to remember that whether we refer to the building or growing of the church, Christ is in command.

Christ declared himself as the builder, as well as the architect (see Hebrews 11:10). The master builder, the one who edifies, and promotes growth. Churches should not focus on growth. In fact, sometimes God purges prior to progress. Spiritual principles of church growth is often misunderstood in new-aged churches. Focusing on growth can box out God's plan.

According to scripture, five-fold ministry is the tool God uses to build, lift up and edify – even still, increase is produced only by God (see Isaiah 41:21). Extreme admiration of church services, key ministries or lead personalities is not God's method of growing the church. In fact, this concept of connecting to followers and supporters is modern day idolatry. It's natural to love and admire your leader. However, this measure of respect should be kept in perspective. The art of discipleship requires that we teach disciples the importance of staying focused on God. This process is challenging. Throughout the process of ministering amongst one another we unknowingly inspire individuals to focus on our strengths as opposed to God's glory. We must be care not to fall prey to this reality.

As disciples, our role is to edify through tongues and build one another up through prophecy. The art of discipleship requires us to stand in the gap supporting individuals and giving them the tools to stand strong in Christ. All too often, emphasis are placed on growth. On the contrary, believers are in desperate need of being taught and securely grounded, which is discipleship. Always remember, Christ promotes growth. In so much, that under difficult circumstances we are instructed not to debate, compromise or argue. "And whosoever shall not receive you, nor hear your words, when ye depart out of that house or city, shake off the dust of your feet" (Matthew 10:14).

Ultimately, God puts us in position to grow. If the body does not grow, or if it grows too much, there is sickness or disease. We must ask ourselves why isn't it growing? Obesity is as much a concern as anorexia for healthy development. Being overweight is equally as damaging to the body as being underweight. When the body gains excessive weight, the outcome is not considered growth, this is called unhealthy fat. Spiritual growth is complicated; this is why God himself orchestrates it for his church. It's common for people to fail to realize that purging is a part of growing. Oftentimes, people understand the need to lose weight physically, while failing to recognize the need for weight gain when necessary. We must remain in position for God to use us in the growth process.

As a believer, when we disciple others, never attempt to replace or substitute God's original plan. Avoid trying to assume ownership of the church. Christ has all power, and our plans will not prevail without him.

His plan is simple, "Go and teach all nations." Another translation says, "Make disciples," which means the way disciples are made is by teaching. This process is similar to coaching men and women using the principles of God's word. A Disciple is a student or learner.

Discipleship requires a God-centered approach. Churches that do not have Christ-centered teachings are merely social clubs. Christ must remain the center of attention as the chief corner stone. God does not need our permission to do anything, although he gives us freewill concerning everything. No matter what art forms, liberties or new-aged theologies we incorporate into our churches, they will never redefine God's original plan for the church. According to Matthew chapter 16, "The gates of hell will not prevail against the church." Strong disciples set captives free by preaching deliverance at the gates of hell (see Isaiah 61:1 and Luke 8:4,18). Our commission takes courage, commitment, knowledge and discipline.

God commands the art of discipleship amongst every individual believer. Although our individual personalities are not intended to redefine the church experience. Our divine directive as disciples develops into a beautiful portrait of believers empowering one another to serve.

CHRIST COACHING TIP

IDD: (Individual Drills) This is when individuals work on their individual positions. Everyone works on their individual skillset, based on the team position they play. IDD is key, because we must have the ability and desire to work on ourselves. In the process of working on ourselves we become better expressions of the gifts we've been created to display.

NOTES
"Write the vision and make it plain" (Habakkuk 2:2)
Chapter 1: The Art of Discipleship

DISCIPLESHIP, *The Catch with Coaching Christians*

Chapter 2
TRANSFORMATION OF A DISCIPLE
Fishermen to Fishers of Men

Transforming from fisherman to fishers of men is imperative for every disciple. As disciples we are students. The suffix "ship" in discipleship defines "the state of a thing or the flow of thing". Using the vernacular of the word ship implies a vessel on water. Discipleship is the time spent in a role to get into the flow of becoming a disciple. This transformation process requires that Christ be understood as the subject and the teacher. According to Hebrews 10:1-7, Christ comes in the volume of the book. Christ is the word made flesh, he is the expressed thought of what is in the book (see Luke 4:1-44).

After his 40-day wilderness experience, Christ returned to the synagogues working miracles and preaching (teaching). Teaching is an assignment for disciples. Transformation is more important than multiplication. Discipleship is not about church growth – it is all about inspiring a life-altering impact. There are so many people who attend church services weekly, but have not been converted into disciples. Like Christ, every disciple needs a wilderness experience – there are many benefits, the most obvious is that the wilderness defines us.

We must thirst after the word of God – this requires us to press. The word press signifies a sense of intense hot urgency. When people pray, praise and prophesy without a press, the process is ineffective. The press is the diligent desire and determination to gain intimacy with God. When pressing we are destined to encounter resistance. Anything that does not speak toward to the brightness and glory of God, does not reflect the press. Disciples always press toward the mark, because our aim is to please God.

Someone may ask the valid question, "What does this transformation look like?" "What exactly am I supposed to look like as a transformed disciple, as opposed to being a traditional church goer?" We cannot ignore the importance of holiness. Living a life with as little sin as possible, all the while knowing you'll never be perfect, is a difficult balancing act.

The Bible best defines this balancing act in Romans chapter 5 and 6. The Apostle Paul writes in Romans chapter 5, that our belief in God covers us with his righteousness. God's righteousness positions us in right standings with him. Seemingly, on the contrary, in Romans chapter 6, he states, "Shall we continue in sin that grace may abound, God forbid." In essence, this conundrum is about intention. Intentionally sinning against God is not acceptable.

What is sin? What does sin look like? Paul writes the church at Philippians, referencing in 3:13-14, "Brethren, I count not myself to have apprehended, but this one thing I do, forgetting those things which are behind and reaching forth unto those things which are before, I press toward the mark of the prize of the high calling which is in Christ Jesus." Throughout my life, one primary explanation of sin is described as missing the mark. What is the mark? Depending on what church you attend or which doctrine you follow, the mark appears to be a moving target. However, religious opinions do not dictate God's intentions. There are so many opinions on what's wrong, what's right, what's sin, and what's not. Paul writes in Romans 3, for all have sinned, and come short of the Glory of God. He helps readers to understand what this mysterious mark is. The mark we are pressing for is the glory of God.

The Greek word for *glory* is Doxa, meaning to honor, praise and worship. Doxa pertains to opinion, reputation, splendor and brightness. In other words, anything that does not bring glory to God is missing the mark. If it does not strengthen the opinion of God or his reputation it is missing the mark. If it is missing the mark it is sin.

Moses missed the mark of the promised land because he did not sanctify God in the eyes of the people. In others words, Moses had a chance to bring glory to God speaking to the rock. Instead he struck the rock. When we strike against God's revelation and his identity we sin. In order for God to make a disciple out of us the prerequisite is not perfection. Godly transformation consists of the following steps:

1. Get out of the flow that we've been used to.
2. Eliminate the fisherman mentality and transform us into fishers of men.

Disciples are like men who catch fish. Jesus taught his disciples how to catch fish using unconventional tactics and timing (see Luke chapter 5). It's important to note that God perfected their profession as fishermen when he transformed their identity as fishers of men. God always makes us better and brings out the best in us. Christ is the anointed one who causes us to see things differently and produce miraculous results. The disciples had been toiling (fishing) all night and caught no fish. When Christ prepares to transform Peter into a disciple, he is previously known as a fisherman. Like Peter, prior to transformation we labor tirelessly and become weary of the world. Transformation turns worldly toiling into spiritual productivity. The carnal mind is unable to comprehend the supernatural. Fishermen have a unique skillset and knowledge, but no revelation. Everything changes when we become fishers of men – embrace the transformation.

> **CHRIST COACHING TIP**
>
> **WEIGHT TRAINING:** During the off-season, the resistance of weights transforms the body to perform at maximum potential. Resistance requires a press. Consistency is what allows the transformation to occur.

NOTES
"Write the vision and make it plain" (Habakkuk 2:2)
Chapter 2: Transformation of a Disciple

DISCIPLESHIP, *The Catch with Coaching Christians*

Chapter 3
YOU ARE NOT ALONE
The Great Commission

We are all commanded to participate in the great commission. Phonics is an important tool for understanding the theology of this commission. For example, scholars refer to this call of discipleship as believers taking action on the earth (see Mathew 28:18-20). Let's consider the word commission. The prefix "co" or "com" is of Latin origin – it means together, mutually or in common. The great commission is meant for us to accomplish together.

In the beginning, God declares that it is not good for man to be alone. The action God commands usually requires teamwork. In the New Testament, disciples were sent out two-by-two (see Luke 10:1). In addition to the disciples NT instructions, the OT prophet Elijah understood God's concept of teamwork. He anointed Jehu and Hazeal, because the work was too much for him to do alone. A similar account of delegated authority takes place when God instructed Moses to pick 70 elders (see Numbers 11:1-17). God's plan for ministry has remained unaltered since the beginning of creation. It takes more than one person to fulfill God's plan - it's certainly takes two.

You are not alone, and don't allow unwanted cycles, circumstances and conflicts to isolate you into thinking that you are. Even amid disagreements, we are encouraged to solicit the support of a spiritual-minded third party for resolution (see Matthew 18:16). Out of the mouth of two or three witnesses every word is established. God desires unity. "Not forsaking the assembling of ourselves together as the manner of some is" (Hebrews 10:25). When we come together, agreement is the expected outcome.

God uses the power of agreement to establish all things. According to Matthew 18:19-20, where two or three have gathered in his name, he will show up. As it relates to our giving and charity, God says, "give and it shall be given unto you, *shall men pour into your bosom*" (Luke 6:38). The most important aspect of this scripture is what readers regularly overlook. The focus of this scripture is that people, not God, will transfer wealth into your life. We need fellowship and love from one another, just like we need God.

Immediately after Christ designates Peter and his friends for transformation, unity becomes the first lesson for disciples. In fact, God says, "By this, shall all men know that you are my disciples, because you have love one for another" (John 13:35). So, God's first lesson is unity, while the enemy's first strategy is division. God commands love, while the enemy causes confusion. God gives the gift of agreement, while the enemy stirs gossip and backbiting. God has been trying to open our eyes to see that we cannot do ministry alone, while the enemy tries to isolate us into thinking that we can conquer the world by ourselves. After transformation, unity is a prerequisite for discipleship.

Remember, one should not attempt to accomplish this work alone. God never gave us a mission, he always commissions. When trees are initially rooted in the ground, gardeners position poles nearby on each side, securing the tree with ropes for support. These poles prevent newly planted trees from falling when pushed, swayed by strong winds or bad storms. This is what our lives should looks like as disciples – we should be positioned to secure the safe transformation and indoctrination of fellow disciples.

It's so important who you surround yourself with. There could be one individual standing in between your success or failure. The difference has lot to do with what vessels are around you. Although Jesus preached from one vessel, the nearby boat was filled with fish also. Preaching alone isn't the only aspect that makes us fishers of men, our connections play a key role in the lives we impact.

The ultimate key to catching fish is encouraging them to believe you are truly an ally – and being an ally. A sense of genuine unpretentious love should be first nature in a disciple's life. That nature is marked by the reality that we are one body of believers. The hand does not say to the head, I don't need you, and neither should we have the attitude that any one individual is not important to the kingdom of God. Religion, church and theology are insignificant if we do not demonstrate love toward one another.

> **CHRIST COACHING TIP**
>
> **TEAM TIME:** This is when the team comes together to work on the overall game plan. The involvement of all players practicing together incorporating warm-up, IDD (Individual Drills) and EDD (Everyday Drills) to become a better team.

NOTES
"Write the vision and make it plain" (Habakkuk 2:2)
Chapter 2: You Are Not Alone

DISCIPLESHIP, *The Catch with Coaching Christians*

Chapter 4
THE ASSIGNMENT
Gap Fillers

Gap fillers are servants in ministry. As a result, we cannot take a high-minded approach or portray an arrogant disposition. Instead, the assignment of a disciple demands unprecedented humility and a gentle sense of assertiveness. Without these characteristics we will not be able to fulfill our assignment.

Ultimately, a disciple is one who sits at the feet of Jesus. Our goal is to intimately know him – this is God's desire – and it should be ours. As disciples we are always pupils. In term, God uses us a foot soldiers; we are sitting, preparing and waiting on our next assignment. The more connected to Christ, the greater the assignment. Our continued relationship with Christ, renovation of our old thoughts, and repentance is the process of how we renew our minds. Repentance far exceeds an apology for sin, it is literally a willingness to change the way one has been thinking. Sitting at the feet of Christ, is an expression for becoming one with his reality by renewing our minds (see Romans 12:2).

Be careful not to overthink God's assignments. Carnal minded concepts are sure to diminish our duties. Our flesh is a serious distraction. Our own minds can become our worse enemies if we allow it. The mind, as in logos or logic can cause philosophical obstacles that roadblock us from fulfilling God's perfect plan. According to Jeremiah 1:5, "We knew him, but not in our flesh." God is a spirit. In order to truly know him, our first assignment requires a renovation of the heart and the renewing of the mind.

God is not flesh. He revealed himself in an earthly body to teach us by example how to fulfill our destiny of discipleship. He teaches us through situations and experiences. His journey allows us to see and learn how to be more like him. Becoming more like him is a daily assignment of every disciple. We should always ask ourselves the spiritually orientated question, "What would Jesus do?"

The daily assignment of all disciples is to consistently examine ourselves based on the word of God. The following three points are examples of a personal examination:

1. Hunger
2. Love vs. Law
3. Work

Hunger is a feeling of weakness or discomfort caused by the lack of eating or the desire to eat. According to Luke 6, Christ and his disciples were in the field, trying to address their issue of hunger. This was an underlined message of their assignment. Disciples must know that there are hungry people in need of God's word. Matthew 5:6 says, "Blessed are they that do hunger and thirst after righteousness for they shall be filled." Also, Christ fed the multitude with two fish and five loaves of bread (see John 6:1-14). Likewise, he commissions us to do the same, "If you love me, feed my sheep" (John 21:17). God will never leave your spirit hungry if you are willing to taste and see that he is good.

As the disciples sat in the presence of Christ, they plucked corn in effort to eat. Christ used this experience to teach the disciples how to deal with the issue of *spiritual* hunger. When persecuted for plucking corn on the Sabbath, Christ reminded the Pharisees that King David ate bread off the altar. This bread was for priests, not kings. Although David did eat and gave the same bread to those that were with him. The lesson in this assignment taught the disciples the importance of always fulfilling the need. Therefore, in order to understand our assignment toward those that hunger and thirst, we too, must experience hunger. Afterward, we will be able to put hunger in the proper perspective, as it relates to God's love verses the laws of the old covenant.

Love verses the law is a continued theme of the New Testament. Many people had an issue with the work of ministry taking place on the Sabbath. According to their perspective, this deed violated the law. Every disciple must understand love verses law. David's response to hunger provides proof that God has always esteemed love over laws. According to Galatians 5:22, against love there is no law. Christ's pure love will always supersede law in effort to accommodate weakness and hunger (see Mark 12:29-31). Ultimately, love is an action that requires work – loving people is our new commandment.

The work required to pull the chaff off for food posed a concerned for religious onlookers. However, God also works. David said, "When When I consider thy heavens, the work of thy fingers, the moon and the stars, which thou hast ordained..." (Psalms 8:3). Work is part of God's plan for mankind. If a man does not work, according to the Bible, he should not eat (see II Thessalonians 3:10). The devil doesn't want you to eat nor work. Working and eating works hand-in-hand. The work of the ministry for a disciple always includes the assignment of feeding sheep. Even spiritually, our next season of work will determine what we eat.

Finally, the assignment of disciples requires a labor of love. Christ did not come to do away with the law, he came to fulfill it. The law had gaps. It wasn't enough. The law left people hungry, dying, and heading to hell. Like Christ, our commission is to do the work that the law couldn't do. This is why disciples are gap fillers. God multiplies the works of our hands.

> **CHRIST COACHING TIP**
>
> EDD: (Everyday Drills) Like IDDs, EDDs is position orientated work. However, it interlaces more players from the team. These drills are based upon things that the team wants to accomplish. These are things that are key to the success of the team. Therefore, they are worked on daily to insure that the team is well versed in these areas.

NOTES
"Write the vision and make it plain" (Habakkuk 2:2)
Chapter 4: The Assignment

DISCIPLESHIP, *The Catch with Coaching Christians*

Chapter 5
CHARACTERISTICS OF A DISCIPLE
Conquering the Climb

Your personal attributes will determine the characteristics you reproduce. Every aspect of discipleship promotes organic spiritual growth in God's Kingdom, churches, and assemblies. All organisms go through mitosis, growth and cell cloning as exact replicas of themselves. This is exactly how the characteristics of a disciple is established.

In Matthew 5, Christ shows us the characteristics disciples should pattern themselves after. Disciples focus on the masses, face challenges, and climb mountains. The following explanations define attributes of discipleship:

1. Disciples are focused on on the masses: Christ saw multitudes. He envisioned his ministry drawing huge crowds. When you are doing real ministry and Christ is centered, ministry has the ability to draw. Christ is the anointed one – when Christ is lifted he draws all men unto himself (see John 12:32). Do not focus on growth – God already has a plan.

2. Disciples face challenges: Christ never allows dedicated disciples to remain comfortable. Every time you think you've done well, God's word will challenge us to go

higher. With progress comes progression – building good character is an ongoing process. God speaks from the mountain – position yourself in the high place to hear his voice – the proper place of worship will require sacrifice.

3. Disciples are mountain climbers: Christ climbed the mountain, and those that were his apprentices climbed with him. The struggle we face with ministry concerning large groups is that people do not want to climb. Going higher equips us to hear him and know him. The masses do not know him. As a result, many churchgoers will have to deal with the consequences of not knowing him (Mathew 7:21-23).

When Christ speaks to his disciples from the mountain top, we refer to this experience as the beatitudes, which means blessed. This particular Greek work blessed means supremely happy. In other scriptures, the words *blessed* means to speak well of. God's plan is to prosper us and bring us to an expected end – he wants us to be happy. The characteristics expected of disciples can seem unfair and overwhelming. Yet, God expects disciples to be exceptional, peculiar and royal.

The primary characteristic of a disciple is supreme and unfailing happiness. Miserable complaining people do not fit the characteristic of a disciple. We even have the God-given ability to think ourselves happy (Acts 26:2). For example, he even encourages us to be happy about being poor in spirit. When we are at the end of our ropes, his strength is made perfect in our weakness. God expects our character to count it all joy when we are persecuted and spoken evil of. Throughout our difficulties, we are instructed to rejoice, not complain, retreat or express defeat. As a result, a carnal-minded person could never be an effective disciple.

Our challenge is to be positive, spiritual-minded, and a servant amongst believers. Even when people are not interested in discipleship, our position must remain steadfast. Instead, far too many believers are only interested in church membership. The two are not the same. As disciples, these characteristics point to the fact we are the light of the world and salt of the earth. Like light, disciples offer exposure, a path, and generates growth. Like salt, we preserve the principles of God word. These are the characteristics that support discipleship.

CHRIST COACHING TIP

PRACTICE MAKES PERFECT: One of the most important principles of coaching is practice. Tedious undesirable repetitive practices are necessary to become better athletes. Practice is not just about getting it right; it is based creating muscle memory. Good habits demand 21 reps – repetition is key to mastery.

NOTES
"Write the vision and make it plain" (Habakkuk 2:2)
Chapter 5: Characteristics of a Discipleship

DISCIPLESHIP, *The Catch with Coaching Christians*

Chapter 6
EXAMINATION OF A DISCIPLE
Staying Spiritual in the Storm

DISCIPLESHIP, *The Catch with Coaching Christians*

How does discipleship fit in God's scheme for our lifestyle? According to Matthew 8:23-28, "If any many will come after me and follow me" suggests that man must be led somewhere. In Genesis chapter 3, man is led away from God's presence and loses fellowship. This is why we need Godly leadership, such as disciples. Reconciliation, intercession and advocation are examples of how disciples leads.

The difficulty with leading people spiritually is coping with carnal rebellion. The flesh or logic of individuals often creates resistance. It is important for people to think for themselves to avoid the brainwash of cult-like religious leaders. However, these thoughts must align with the mind of Christ. "Let this mind be in you, which was also in Christ Jesus" (Philippians 2:5). Disciples surrender their own logic, crucify the flesh daily, and adopt the mind of Christ. The flesh has to go through a demolition process. It has to be destroyed. According to the scripture, the flesh must die daily (I Corinthians 15:31).

Christ says, if any man will be his disciple he must deny himself, take up his cross, and then follow. This means we must possess a willingness to suffer for and with him. We must understand the hypostatic union. As a man, he is able to intercede because he understands, as God he keeps us from falling.

When Christ tell his disciples, "Let's cross over to the other side," they were about to go through a self-evaluation, according to Mark 4:34. Tests are what I call examinations. The concept of a *test* is often seen as intimidating challenges, but God is not interested in nerve-wracking experiences. God's desire is to send us through a process of self-examination. This examination is not based on where they were positioned in life, but where they were going. In essence, the devil's plan concerning our lives is to obstruct us from God's promises and cause us to miss the mark. Complacency is a mark of the enemy, because he wants you to stay stuck where you are. The disciples were about to deal with demons. Every crossover has a new set of enemies. Stop talking about your haters and learn how to take authority over the forces that are using them.

Notice how disciples will follow their leader into a storm. We must examine ourselves by asking, "Am I willing to follow? We can't afford to be carnal-minded when you are about to crossover. When crossing over, the waves covered the ship. As vessels used by God, we will sometimes feel like we are drowning in despair. Always remember, boats (vessels) need water in order to crossover, and water represents the word of God (see Ephesians 5:25-26). The very thing we must face in order to crossover to our promised possession can be intimidating – waves are fierce. Water can be as fierce as it can be peaceful. Yet, Christ instructed them to get in the water and crossover – sending them in the direction of the storm.

They took issue with the fact that the waves covered them. When something covers you, you're unable to see your surroundings. Also, whatever is surrounding you is unable to see you. The Bible records it this way, "He that dwelleth in the secret place of the most High shall abide under the shadow of the Almighty" (Psalms 91:1). Since water represents the word of God, when we are crossing over, we have no need to be afraid. Notice how at the scariest moment of their lives, Christ was at peace and sound asleep.

This difficult exam taught them how to see one thing with their eyes and receive another thing within their spirit. The truth is, God never sleep nor slumbers. When you focus on the flesh, you'll think otherwise, but God is a spirit always and all the time. Discipleship is the kind of art form that leads people to see the beauty in God.

CHRIST COACHING TIP

MIND OVER MATTER:

There will be circumstances when your team is running out of time, trailing the opponent and tired. Despite exhaustion, you cannot quit, you must stay focused, passed this test and win the game. Train your mind to only focus on what matters.

NOTES
"Write the vision and make it plain" (Habakkuk 2:2)
Chapter 6: Examination of a Discipleship

DISCIPLESHIP, *The Catch with Coaching Christians*

DISCIPLESHIP, *The Catch with Coaching Christians*

DISCIPLESHIP, *The Catch with Coaching Christians*

www.ingramcontent.com/pod-product-compliance
Lightning Source LLC
Chambersburg PA
CBHW031614040426
42452CB00006B/514